THE WORLD
ACCORDING TO

CHRISTIAN
DOR

Edited by
Patrick Mauriès
Jean-Christophe Napias

Foreword by
Patrick Mauriès

Illustrations and design by
Isabelle Chemin

T&H

First published in the United Kingdom in 2022 by
Thames & Hudson Ltd, 181A High Holborn, London WC1V 7QX

First published in the United States of America in 2022 by
Thames & Hudson Inc., 500 Fifth Avenue, New York, New York 10110

Reprinted 2024

The World According to Christian Dior
© 2022 Thames & Hudson Ltd, London

Edited compilation © 2022 Patrick Mauriès and Jean-Christophe Napias
Foreword © 2022 Patrick Mauriès

Illustrations and design by Isabelle Chemin

Quotations reproduced from *Je suis couturier* © 1951 Christian Dior, and
Conférences écrites par Christian Dior pour la Sorbonne © 1955–1957 Christian
Dior, translated from the French language by Thames & Hudson,
with kind permission from the Dior Estate.

Quotations reproduced from *Christian Dior et moi* © 1956 Christian Dior and
Petit dictionnaire de la mode © 1954 Christian Dior translated from the French
language by Thames & Hudson, with kind permission from the Dior Estate and
V&A publishing, a division of V&A Enterprises Ltd.

Illustrations on p.114 and p.142 based on original illustrations by Christian Dior.
Reproduced with the kind permission of the Dior Estate.

The authors would like to thank Jérôme Gautier, Soizic Pfaff,
Perrine Scherrer, Solène Auréal, Jennifer Walheim and Joana Tosta
at Dior for their invaluable help in the making of this book.

All Rights Reserved. No part of this publication may be reproduced or
transmitted in any form or by any means, electronic or mechanical, including
photocopy, recording or any other information storage and retrieval system,
without prior written permission from the publisher.

British Library Cataloguing-in-Publication Data
A catalogue record for this book is available from the British Library

Library of Congress Control Number 2021943176

ISBN 978-0-500-02414-0

Printed and bound in China by C&C Offset Printing Co. Ltd

MIX
Paper | Supporting
responsible forestry
FSC® C008047
www.fsc.org

Be the first to know about our new releases,
exclusive content and author events by visiting
thamesandhudson.com
thamesandhudsonusa.com
thamesandhudson.com.au

CONTENTS

THE THREE DIORS

On 12 February 1947, at around ten o'clock in the morning, a fragrance with light floral notes drifted unseasonably across the avenue Montaigne, which was freezing in the winter cold. A couturier, unknown to the public at large, had waited until the final day of the season's fashion shows to present his first collection and to launch a perfume with a floral bouquet. On his demand, the scent had been sprayed throughout the salons, creating an anticipatory, subliminal, sensual aroma that spilled out onto the street.

That morning was the moment that Christian Dior stepped out, literally, from obscurity into the spotlight; in which he saw himself lauded by the shrewd and formidable editor of *Harper's Bazaar*, Carmel Snow, with her famous remark: 'your dresses have such a new look!' (which the author Colette immediately transcribed into French rather cheekily as '*nioulouque*'). But it could also be seen as a seminal moment for what would become, even up until the present day, standard for the fashion world: a partnership between a designer and a businessman (Dior was then only the servant of the textile magnate who financed him, Marcel Boussac), the dawn of mass media, the internalization of style, the building of a brand and, ultimately, the mythification of the figure of the couturier, definitively elevated above the level of mere vendor.

The fame of Jacques Doucet, Paul Poiret, Coco Chanel and Jeanne Lanvin was built up over time, by capitalizing on the novelty of their designs and a network of recommendations and recognition from a wealthy clientele, whose members moved in elite circles: social, literary and artistic, Parisian as well as international. Dior himself was no stranger to these circles, which makes his case even more exemplary. In fact, he was a liminal figure, straddling two different definitions of society and of fashion; he was also the first designer whose life and work was shared through what we would now call a 'media event', making him more or less a consenting participant in a new economy – in a loose sense – the emergence of which had been prefigured by others, including Lucien Lelong. (Indeed Dior had left his job as a designer at Lelong to found his own house.)

A son of the conservative provincial bourgeoisie, indelibly influenced by the fragrances and froufrou of the Belle Époque, the young Christian Dior socialized with the bohemians of Paris, befriending a student at the Académie Ranson, the artist Christian Bérard, whom he would meet up with after class. He became part of a mixed circle where society luminaries, such as the Beaumonts and the Noailles, rubbed shoulders with artists, writers and poets – the ubiquitous Jean Cocteau, Max Jacob, Julien Green, Marcel Jouhandeau and René Crevel, among others. He became particularly close to several young painters, friends and frenemies of Bérard – the Eugene brothers, Leonid Berman, the shadowy Pavel Tchelitchew – who left their mark on history under the rather inadequate label of 'neo-Romantics'.

Along with a few other artists then at the beginning of their careers (Dalí, Giacometti, Jean and Valentine Hugo), they would play a crucial role in the first stage of Dior's life, which was as an art dealer. With the financial help of his father (given only on the condition that the family name should not appear in the name of the business, due to their high social standing), Dior opened his first gallery in 1928, with one of his friends, Jacques Bonjean. Three years later, after

Bonjean had fallen on hard times, he partnered with the young Pierre Colle, a member of Max Jacob's circle. Despite their initial success, the business soon failed, laid low by the repercussions of the stock market crash of 1929 and family financial troubles.

What followed was a decade or so of various jobs that served as a series of prologues to his future career, including – before he joined Lelong – a role as a designer at the fashion house of the elegant Robert Piguet. A meeting with Marcel Boussac in 1945 marked the beginning of the final phase of a life that was strangely divided into three stages, and eventually punctuated by Dior's early death on 24 October 1957, only a decade after the opening of his fashion house.

Those ten years were marked by a series of 'lines' – Corolle, Ailée, Tulipe, Muguet, H, A, Y, Fuseau, and more – which altered, redrew and redefined the lines of the body (it is no coincidence that he made another master of line, René Gruau – heir of Toulouse-Lautrec, that icon of fin-de-siècle Paris who had so influenced him – his illustrator of choice). The term 'line' belongs just as much to the lexicon of art and graphic design as it does to fashion, and thus signals a continuity from one phase of the couturier's life to the next – in other words, from one Dior to another. It is also a leitmotif in several interviews and written works, including two autobiographical volumes: *Christian Dior et moi* and *Je suis couturier* (although shy, the creator of the New Look had plenty to say) in which Dior speaks often of the difference between the identities of 'Christian', the timid aesthete with unerring taste, and 'Dior', a flamboyant and fictional figure. The latter cannot be understood without the former, the one who is often forgotten. While he did not always have the same unfailing instinct for snappy but sometimes simplistic phrases as Chanel, Dior possessed a simplicity and an authenticity that is showcased in the pages that follow. A nostalgic and a dreamer, he was able to capture the spirit of an era and make an unquestionable mark on history, yet without compromising his lifelong vision and aesthetics. 'I'm a mild man,' he summed up wittily, 'but I have violent tastes.'

Patrick Mauriès

CHRISTIAN ACCORDING TO DIOR

I used to look at women, I would admire their figures and I was aware of their elegance, like all boys of my age; but I would have been utterly amazed if anyone had ever predicted that one day I would become a couturier; that I would study in minute detail the craft of cutting, stretching and draping fabrics.

★

I learned through instinct. Sometimes it was very difficult. It's by working that you learn the different possibilities of a fabric: drapery, straight grain and bias cut. The more dresses I made, the more I learned.

★

Coming so late, with no apprenticeship but my own intuition and no method other than necessity, to a craft where one learns something every day, I've always had worries about never quite knowing enough. Perhaps it was this fear of always being an amateur that helped to sweep away my final doubts and compel me to invent the character of Christian Dior?

An unintentional couturier, I would be ungrateful and most of all inaccurate if I did not begin my story with the word

LUCK

written in capital letters.

There are two Christian Diors, *myself* **and the other one,** and they are increasingly separate.

He and I have a score to settle.

It's me who was born in Granville in the département *of Manche, on 21 January 1905, to Alexandre-Louis-Maurice Dior, an industrialist, and Madeleine Martin, of no profession. Half-Parisian, half-Norman, I'm very devoted – although I never go back there – to the land where I was born. I like intimate gatherings of close friends; I hate noise, the bustle of society and any kind of sudden change.*

It's he who is the great couturier. He's the boutique on the avenue Montaigne and all the buildings that surround it. He is a thousand people, gowns, stockings, perfumes, advertisements on billboards, photographs in the press, and, every once in a while, a minor revolution in which no blood (but plenty of ink) is spilled, and whose aftershocks can be felt on the other side of the world.

★

The smallest things separate us. He lives entirely in his own century and owes everything to that; he prides himself on being revolutionary, or at the very least, dazzling. I was born into a bourgeois family, who were conscious of being so and proud of it.

In everyday life, something unfortunate happens to a lot of people when they acquire a little bit of fame: they become like storybook characters, with people telling stories about them which get embroidered and exaggerated. When in fact most people's lives, whether they are famous or not, remain very much the same, and they continue to lead a simple existence that consists primarily of work, a great deal of work, and professional dedication.

★

Should I have transformed myself so as not to disappoint my public? Should I have resorted to weight-loss regimes and given up not only my gourmandise, but everything that gives pleasure in my life? I gave up the idea almost immediately. The gap between the way I ought to have looked and myself was too wide. With relief, I resigned myself to being simply what I was by nature, and to which, over the years, I have become accustomed.

Other than the fact that I never liked seeing myself in pictures, I felt that my presence as a rotund gentleman, always dressed in the neutral colours of a

Parisian from Passy,

would never resemble the pin-up-boys or the decadent Petronius figures that are the standard image of

fashionable couturiers.

Ultimately, all that I know, see and hear – everything in my life – is expressed in dresses. Dresses are my dreams, but gentle dreams that have moved out of the realm of fantasy and into the world of everyday items designed to be worn.

★

I saw the exercise of my craft as a kind of battle against everything in our times that is mediocre and demoralizing.

★

The fierceness and focus I put into my work perhaps betray, above all, my desire to get it finished quickly.

★

Fashion has its own life and its own reasons that reason cannot explain. For me, I merely know what I owe to my gowns: care, worry, passion; they are nothing less than the reflection of my day-to-day existence, with its emotions and its surges of affection and joy. While some disappointed or deceived me, others loved me as faithfully as I loved them. I can truly say that my most exciting and passionate affairs have been with my gowns. I am obsessed with them. They preoccupy me, then occupy me, and eventually post-occupy me, if I may dare to coin the term…

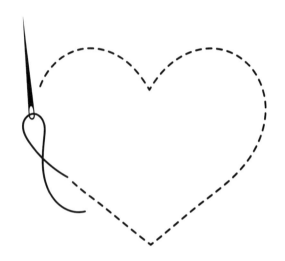

This craft can only be done
with love. You have to
put your whole

heart

into it.

The first
applause
is always
a source
of fear.

Success is nothing but work and more work.

★

Where does success come from? I can never predict it. Will it rise from the path you might expect, the path of audacity and true novelty? Or quite the opposite, will the public baulk at what I like best and praise other designs instead? Or will they remain indifferent? This is the catastrophe that has so often haunted my nights.

★

In general, the designs that I find exciting unsettle the public; the eye has to grow accustomed to them.

★

Some gowns, made with love, are met with indifference, while others, made only with skill, are warmly applauded. With the pleasures of a great success come a certain bitterness and a few little disappointments.

ACCESSORIES
ACCORDING TO
DIOR

When you create a line, a silhouette, I believe it must go from head to toe. From hats to shoes, via gloves and bags.

There are potentially hundreds of people with the same scarf as you: it's your way of wearing it that makes it unique! Exclusivity is not a matter of price.

Accessories are a charming addition – but always the least possible for the best effect.

Shoes are very important, because immediately after the face, it's what people look at.

You can never be too careful about your choice of shoes. Too many women think they're not very important, but it's by her feet that you can judge whether a woman is elegant or not.

**HIGH
HEELS**
ARE
AN
INVALUABLE
PEDESTAL.

I am rather
sorry to see
that women do
not wear hats
as much as they
once did. After
all, the first thing
you see when you
look at a person
is their face and
a hat is truly part
of the face.

I believe a woman without a hat isn't fully dressed.

★

*Buy more hats than clothes. Because hats make
for gaiety.*

★

*A hat is the quintessence of femininity, with all
the frivolity that those words bring to mind.*

★

*It would be wrong for women not to use such an
effective weapon of flirtation.*

★

*Among my early designs, the ideas for hats were very
successful. My designs for gowns were much less so,
and that's probably one of the reasons why I worked
so hard to make sure they were well made.*

★

*It would be impossible for me to show a collection
without hats: the models, even if they were wearing
the most beautiful gown in the world, would
somehow seem naked.*

COLOUR
ACCORDING TO
DIOR

Gentlemen prefer... colours.

Any colour, as delightful as it may be, would lose its effect if you wore it every day. Colour brings renewal. Would we appreciate the blue of the sky if it were always blue?

With the exception of a few artworks that defined my childhood, what I loved doing most was to learn by heart all the names and descriptions of flowers in the colour images of the Vilmorin-Andrieux catalogues.

A collection could be quite persuasively created in black or in white, but why deprive fashion and women of the luxury and charm of colour?

I love
GREY

★

It's the most
practical and
elegant of the
neutral colours.

BATTLEMENT
GREY
MOTH
GREY
WHISPER
GREY
DAWN
GREY
URANIUM
GREY
MARENGO
GREY
ÎLE-DE-FRANCE
GREY
WALK-THROUGH-WALLS
GREY
TRIANON
GREY
MAGNET
GREY

porcelain pink...
whisper pink...
French pink...
frost pink...
Boreal pink...
dusky pink...
flamingo pink...
ibis pink...
pale cloud pink...
peony pink...
firebrand pink...
happy pink...
Indian pink...
begonia pink...
autumn pink...
Rose Bertin pink...
electric pink...

The softest of colours.
Every woman
should have

PINK

in her wardrobe.
It's the colour of
happiness and
femininity.

*Invigorating and attractive, it's the colour of life.
I love red.*

★

*The lipstick marks that cover my cheeks are the
surest sign that a collection is a success; what's
more, red is my lucky colour.*

SCREAM
RED

BLAZING
RED

ZINNIA
RED

DEVIL
RED

MADDER
RED

ARA
RED

EMBER
RED

POPPY
RED

GERANIUM
RED

DIOR
RED

CHRISTMAS
RED

ROYAL
RED

GOYA
RED

People say that green is malevolent. Wrongly, in my opinion. I myself am superstitious, but green has always brought me luck. It's also a very appealing and elegant colour.

Isn't it a colour of nature? And when you use nature as your reference point, you can't really go wrong.

Longchamp green...
Vertigo green...
Aiguevives green...
Aigue-mortes green...
lichen green...
seaweed green...
kelp green...
dawn green...
dusk green...
lawn green...
Irish green...
Spanish moss green...
grass green...
spring green...
Dauphin green...
Turkish green...
winter green...

PARIS **BLUE**... NORDIC **BLUE**...

HUMMINGBIRD **BLUE**...

MACAW **BLUE**... ALTITUDE **BLUE**...

STORM **BLUE**... ORIENTAL **BLUE**...

FLAME **BLUE**... ENAMEL **BLUE**...

FRENCH **BLUE**... ATLANTIC **BLUE**...

HYDRANGEA **BLUE**... DIOR **BLUE**...

VERMEER **BLUE**...

FONTAINEBLEAU **BLUE**...

MARIE ANTOINETTE **BLUE**...

PERSIAN **BLUE**... TYROLEAN **BLUE**...

MAGNETIC **BLUE**...

Of all
colours, only

NAVY
BLUE

can truly
rival black.

Black for any time
of day. The

DEEP BLACK

of velvet and
wool velvet, the

GLOSSY BLACK

of taffetas and
satin, the

MATT BLACK

of wool, grosgrain and faille.

It's so black that it
becomes a colour.

*We call black glorious and we rank it among
the colours, because through fabric contrasts,
ornaments and accessories that accompany it,
it becomes an active element of colour.*

★

*Above all, morning, afternoon and evening, the
blackest black of an ant's shell, which we love as
a colour; the most simple, the most formal and
the most elongating...*

★

*It's the most prized, the most practical and the
most elegant of colours.*

★

*Of all colours, it is the most slimming and, unless
you look unwell, the most flattering.*

The little black dress is vital to any wardrobe.

Black is the ideal colour, no matter what the fabric. If you could only have one gown, I would definitely recommend black.

For its elegance and practicality, a little black suit has no equal.

The French woman is at her best in black – and black is at its best when it is contrasted with one bright colour.

I could write an entire book on black…

A good
**little black
dress**
can never
be beaten.

COUTURE
ACCORDING TO
DIOR

Couture is first and foremost a marriage between form and fabric. People know that many such marriages are blissful, but there are unhappy ones too.

★

Haute couture has at least two basic justifications. First of all, it is a prototype, and, as such, it is expensive. Secondly, it is a triumph of conscientious endeavour, a handcrafted wonder, a sort of masterpiece; it represents hundreds of hours of work. That is its intrinsic value. But it also possesses another, incalculable value. It's like the first raspberry or the first snowdrop. It's ahead of its time and entirely novel. And tomorrow, through the way in which it is worn, it will set a trend for Paris fashion, which is the fashion of the world.

In the age of
the machine,
couture is the
last refuge of
craftsmanship

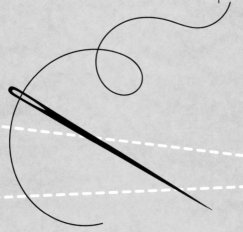

Couture
should
be interested by
life,
always.

I believe that haute couture, if it is to remain haute couture, must never forget that it needs to stay alive. By that, I mean that it must adapt to suit the needs of every modern woman's life and, regardless of its technical quality, it must take care not to become Museum Couture.

★

It has always been part of the mission of Parisian couture to leave well-trodden paths behind and be constantly in renewal.

★

We sell ideas above finished products. The ultimate aim of haute couture is not only to make *but to* create *clothes, to invent new forms, new ways of cutting and using fabrics, to put the New and the Never-Before-Seen on the market in the constantly changing world of fashion; in a sense, it is an immaterial business.*

★

A house of couture is first and foremost a research laboratory.

*Couturiers have a very fine role to play. In
the absence of Cinderella's fairy godmother,
they are the only ones who possess the gift of
transfiguration. And this power would lose a great
deal of its splendour if the transfiguration was
not preceded by great ceremony and expectation.
Lavish gowns, magnificent fanfares and torchlit
celebrations quench some of the thirst for glamour
that lies dormant in everyone.*

*They embody one of the last sanctuaries of the
marvellous. They are, in a sense, the masters
of dreams.*

*The ultimate goal of couture is to embellish rather
than dress, to adorn rather than clothe.*

We are purveyors of ideas.

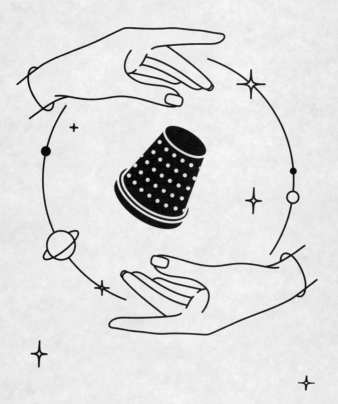

In our world,
which is so
deprived of
wonders, a
couturier is a kind
of magician.

*Paris represents the perfect finished product.
It's where people come from all over the world to
seek out the artisanal quality that cannot be found
anywhere else and that we must above all seek
to preserve.*

★

In Paris, couture is in the air.

★

*Whether French or foreign, everyone understands
that the grand business of Paris couture is not
merely a vanity fair, but a frivolous and dazzling
display from a civilization that is determined
to endure.*

The tradition of **PARIS** is reinvention.

The need for splendour
that lies dormant in all our
hearts – especially at a time when
we are so deprived of it – has
chosen fashion as one of
its supreme solutions.

In times as sombre as ours, in which cannons and four-engined fighter planes are luxury items, our kind of luxury must be resolutely defended. I cannot pretend that this does not run contrary to the way the world seems to be turning. Everything beyond the simple need to find clothing, food and shelter is a luxury. Our civilization is a luxury, and we must defend it.

I often hear it said that fashion is fickle and its creations are wasteful. Those, it seems, are the two major criticisms. I might respond that the latter cancels out the former; better yet, it justifies it.

ELEGANCE
ACCORDING TO
DIOR

The word deserves a book to itself! All I will say is that elegance should be a balance of simplicity, care, naturalness and distinction. Nothing must be added, or else it's no longer a question of elegance but of pretention. Elegance has no connection with wealth.

★

There is almost no woman who has the right to abandon her appearance. To do so is simply lazy. By using her intelligence even the most ordinary woman can create the illusion of beauty.

★

A woman who can only buy one dress generally chooses it with such care that she makes the right choice. For this reason, she achieves elegance more often than women who possess lots of dresses.

Is there a magic key?
That would be too easy, all
you would have to do was
acquire it and all
your worries would
be gone. As it happens,

good taste,
care and
simplicity

– the rudiments of fashion –
cannot be bought. But
they are within reach
of all women.

No elegant woman follows fashion blindly.

★

*A successful garment must be so well balanced
that it seems impossible to change anything.
Every element is vital: that is what style is.*

★

*Elegance may be audacious, but never extravagant.
Extravagance is in bad taste. When dressing,
it's always better to err on the side of too much
simplicity rather than extravagance.*

★

*The art of dressing well is international – as is
elegance.*

When it
comes to
elegance,
details
are as
important
as the
main idea.
When a detail
is wrong,
it spoils
the whole
ensemble.

Being a woman
whose elegance
makes waves
requires

**tradition
and chic**

(which is a heavenly gift
even rarer than beauty)

AND

GREAT
SKILL.

For men, the only kind of elegance is going unnoticed. For women, it means being noticed. They dress for their own enjoyment. And to seduce, of course.

★

It's quite probable that, because I lived in Paris, went out a lot, and mixed in very different circles, a particular concept of elegance must have formed inside me, but it was not until I started designing that I began to look at dresses with the specific aim of understanding why they worked or why they didn't.

Complying with the tricky rules of elegance is a way of acquiring self-discipline, as well as coming to an understanding with everything outside of one's self, the world of other people and the world of things.

★

Fashion is all about emphasizing and elevating the beauty of women.

★

Whatever you're doing – for work or for pleasure – do it with passion! Live with passion… That's the secret of fashion, and the secret of beauty. Beauty can't be seductive without that zest.

Never forget that above all, getting dressed means making oneself beautiful.

WOMEN
ACCORDING TO
DIOR

As a couturier,
I naturally think
of women with
a figure like
Venus. But
when I come
to deal with
reality, I find
great pleasure
in designing
for women who
are less perfect.

My desire is to make women's wishes come true.

★

Women, with their sure instincts, must have understood that I dreamed not only of making them more beautiful but also happier. Their appreciation was my reward.

★

I do not design with a particular woman in mind. I am thinking, as I have said already, of the average woman.

★

As a Parisian couturier, not only do I have to understand the needs of French women, but the needs of elegant women all over the world.

★

I believe that the ideal woman would embody three things: French femininity, English refinement and American polish. I think this would make for a very charming League of Nations.

Throughout history, women have had the delicate desire to please and couturiers have done everything they can to help them.

★

Tall or short, fat or thin, there are very few women who can do nothing with themselves.

★

[When you look at a woman, what do you notice first?] *Her face, and especially her eyes. Then her figure. Then come her powers of diplomacy.*

★

All women should know that simply to be a woman is to have the power to enchant.

WOMEN DON'T
WEAR WHAT
THEY
LIKE,
THEY
LIKE
WHAT THEY
WEAR.

Form is my guide
above all things.
A woman's body
is the foundation,
and the couturier's
art is to build
and scale a set of
three-dimensional
shapes around it
that will glorify
her form.

As I conceive it, a dress is an ephemeral piece of architecture that is designed to celebrate the proportions of the female body. Couturiers consult their plumb lines no less frequently than stonemasons.

A woman's body is a single note with which the couturier can compose a thousand variations, like a musician who has only the seven notes of the scale at his disposition.

One must dress two kinds of women: the ones who have hips and the ones who don't.

I only like slim waists, and I think that most women prefer or dream of having slim waists.

As fashions change – alternating, one after the other – some parts of the body are and our attention shifts and is renewed, as is our attraction. It is fascinating to see the way that, as generations go by, different features are considered to be the object of charm, with relative constants for each generation.

I am against fashions that are not natural. Nature has endowed woman's figure with a bust, a waist and hips. I do not intend to change that.

★

Didn't I say that fashion is a blooming flower? This is a way of saying that fashion is anti-skinniness... just like I myself am anti-diet.

**The waist
is the
central
question
of fashion.**

A weapon
of seduction:
décolletage.

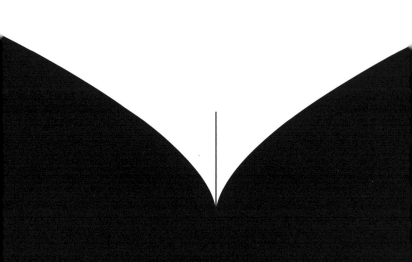

*Personally, I take great care in designing new
styles of décolletage that will suit every woman.
There's nothing more becoming. There's nothing
more feminine. There's nothing more seductive.*

★

*You know, I was born in an era when women were
really women, and I didn't care for the fashions
between the wars, when women were ashamed to
really be women.*

★

*I've always loved a generous chest.
Miss Lollobrigida is the biggest success of our
era and I have great admiration for her.*

★

*I have always made it a rule to emphasize a
different asset of a woman's body as the seasons
change. And of all of them, isn't the bust the most
seductive?*

Is there a woman alive who hasn't lived the Cinderella story and turned into a princess, for at least one night of her life?

★

An attractive woman has no age.

★

If I am particular, even rigorous, in my designs for daytime, then for the night there is no limit to the way I would adorn a woman to make her beautiful.

AFTER
WOMEN,
FLOWERS
ARE THE
MOST
DIVINE OF
CREATIONS.

INSPIRATION
ACCORDING TO
DIOR

I'm often asked where I get my inspiration from; honestly, I don't know. Perhaps a psychoanalyst – who would also be a couturier – could work it out, by studying my series of collections and the emotions of my past life.

Couture is a collection of a thousand and one things. There are a thousand and one crafts that are clustered around the job of the couturier.

It would be wrong to imagine that a new silhouette is born from a mass of research. In most cases, it is born from coincidence, a chance encounter. When you are constantly designing dresses, you start to see them everywhere where they are not. And then, suddenly, like a bolt of lightning, a sketch appears. That's it!

My inspiration is subconscious and vital. I design very quickly, after thinking long and hard. I can't say where fashion springs from, but I can't work in any other way.

**I doodle
everywhere:**
in bed,
in the bath,
at the table,
in the car,
standing up,
in the sunshine,
in lamplight,
by day,
by night.

I know
quite a lot
about art

and I've
seen lots of
paintings;

it's very
possible that
some of it
comes out in
my dresses.

It's what you feel the best that you execute the best.

★

Nothing is invented, you must always begin somewhere.

★

You can paint the same picture several times and build the same house a hundred times, but you can never make the same dress twice in a row. There's no craft – or perhaps I could say art form – that demands such creative exertion.

I thank the heavens for having lived in Paris in the final years of the Belle Époque. They marked me for life.

★

Before, I used to work with paintings, through which painters express their personality. Afterwards, when that stage had passed, I wanted to express myself too, in my own way, and so I began to design dresses.

★

When I'm in the process of designing a dress, I dedicate it to a particular elegant woman. I think it will suit her. This woman isn't necessarily a client of mine, but she's a woman I know.

★

If a couturier today can tell you about his trade, it is because his profession has risen from a craft to a form of artistic creation. His dresses bear his signature, and he seeks to impose his tastes on others. The material, which was once dominant, must now bow before style.

For a dress to be a success, you have to have an idea of what it will be like when it's brought to life by movement.

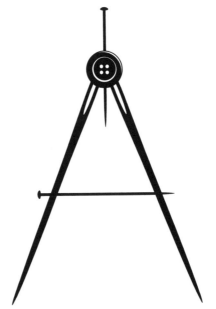

I WANTED TO BE
AN ARCHITECT.
AS A COUTURIER,
I AM OBLIGED TO
FOLLOW THE LAWS
AND PRINCIPLES
OF ARCHITECTURE.

*Proportions are the most important thing. They
must be calculated: the length of a peplum or a
hem must be measured to the centimetre, sometimes
to the millimetre. Couture demands as much
accuracy as architecture.*

*Long before the desire for something well sewn or
well cut, the couturier feels a desire for expression,
and all things being equal, it is possible for
couture to become a means of expression that
can, ephemeral as it is, nevertheless be compared
to architecture or painting. But even if artistic
expression is the primary aim, a collection cannot
be a success unless it is also well cut and well
sewn: just as the most beautiful house is not of
significance unless it is well built.*

*To satisfy my desire for architecture and precise
forms, I wanted my gowns to be built around the
curves of a woman's body, giving her a stylized
silhouette.*

A gown – particularly if it is worn well – is more eloquent than a couturier.

When my gowns are finished, I seem to lose interest in them; I almost never see them again. It's then that they become goods for sale.

A dress is a construction, and it is constructed according to the grain of the fabric. This is the secret of couture, and it is a secret that depends on the first law of architecture: the law of gravity. The way that a fabric falls – and the line and balance of a dress created by this fall – depends on the direction of the grain.

GOWNS SHOULD
HAVE A

soul

AND SHOULD
SAY SOMETHING.

In the studio, every new collection is like the coming of spring and the pieces of fabric are the fresh young shoots.

The way in which the grain of a fabric is utilized, switching direction from one piece to another, is one of the secrets of our trade.

With the same idea and the same fabric, a dress can as easily be a success as a complete failure.

Better to have a single gown made of quality fabric than two made of cheap material.

Fabric is the vehicle for our dreams, and it also feeds our ideas. It can be the departure point for our inspiration. Plenty of gowns are born from fabric alone.

How do you admit to a client that a modest little dress is as labour-intensive as a splendidly draped evening gown?

★

I looked for a fashion that had foundations. Real luxury demands real materials and real craftsmanship.

★

Couture is primarily a marriage between form and fabric. A well-cut dress is a dress with as few cuts as possible: that's one of the biggest secrets of couture.

What is on the inside
is often more important
than what the eye
can see.

THE HOUSE OF DIOR ACCORDING TO DIOR

My idea was to create a house where everything would be new: from its state of mind and its staff to its furniture and its location.

★

With great daring, I described the couture house of my dreams. It would be very small, very select, with the fewest ateliers; people would work there according to the finest couture traditions, aimed at a very elegant clientele. I would only create designs that looked quite simple, but which were extremely complex to make.

★

What was needed was a return to the great luxury tradition of French couture. I imagined that in order to achieve this, the house would – at a time when machines are taking over everywhere – look more like a laboratory of artisans than a factory of fashion.

★

What can I tell you about my house? How can one talk about the present and what one is living through? It is, in effect, my whole life.

A couture house is like someone in poor health. Every day, you have to take its temperature, feel its pulse, measure its blood pressure, carry out tests — in a nutshell, you must behave like a doctor who leaves nothing to chance, no stone unturned.

IN MY COUTURE
HOUSE IN PARIS

I have a
thousand
women,

AND BELIEVE ME,
THAT'S QUITE ENOUGH

for one
man.

You cannot bring together so many talents without also surrounding yourself with unpredictable annoyances and sensitivities. So many ruffles over fabric!

In a profession where everything is a matter of taste, you must constantly take everyone's personality into account, at every level. The petite main *puts a little of her heart and mind into every hem.*

I find it very moving to think that every atelier reflects the personality of a true artist, and it's thanks to them that I can carry out the task that I have set for myself. And what a task!

The true craft is being able to make use of all those hands that cut, assemble, fit, sew and overcast to express everything that you feel and desire.

I risk the salary of nine hundred people in making a collection.

A winter collection is created in the time of lilac and cherry blossom, a summer collection amid falling leaves or the first snowflakes. This distance from the season in which the piece will be worn – which is imposed by production and shipping deadlines – is paradoxically an advantage. It's this that gives our work an element of nostalgia, a longing for sunshine or mist, depending on the season, that makes inspiration sharper.

A collection should
be based on a
fairly small number
of ideas! Ten or
so, at most. You
must know how
to vary them,
explore them,
emphasize them,
impose them.
Around those

TEN IDEAS

the whole
collection is built.

THEY ARE UNBEARABLE AND DELIGHTFUL. THAT'S WHY PEOPLE LOVE THEM. WHAT WOULD THIS CRAFT, FULL OF LIFE AND MOVEMENT, BE LIKE IF EVERYTHING HAD TO BE PRESENTED ON WOODEN MANNEQUINS? I HARDLY DARE TO IMAGINE IT.

Fortunately, a couturier has the best ambassadors in the world on his side: models.

★

The finance department tends to think that I hire too many of them or pay them too much; the premières d'atelier *believe that I let them get away with too much; the* vendeuses *sometimes claim that they're impossible to work with. I say nothing. My models give life to my dresses, and I want my dresses to be happy.*

★

A gown and its model are elements that can be as inseparable as a gown and its fabric.

★

One must distinguish between a top model and an inspiring model. They are not necessarily the same, since I do not see my collection with the same eyes as my audience. A top model projects outwards; she gives a garment prestige, she has to seize the gown and, as we say in the trade, make it sing. An inspiring model projects inwards; she gives expression to my ideas, translating them into silhouette and movement from the first moment of creation.

I believe that couturiers, if they didn't have an audience waiting, would never show their collections and would always find something that needed to be redone – the last moments before a show bring such anxiety and doubt.

★

Fashion is like theatre. You always feel like it's your début when you have to present your dresses.

★

The buzz of admiration and applause that greeted some of my creations were a source of immediate delight that I am certain I will never tire of.

★

It is then, between the moment when the model puts on the gown and when she steps out into the spotlight to present it in the salons, that I get the chance – for the first and also the last time – to truly discover my designs and what they mean. No matter how tired I am, that fleeting instant is almost always a moment of happiness.

★

It's there, in the whirl of congratulations that follow a collection show, that a new fashion begins to be born.

I admit that I feel anxiety, an anxiety that I try to control and to hide, when a show carries on for a while in silence. It is said that silence means people are paying attention, but I prefer applause!

THE BONDS

that join a
designer and
his clients
are a repicrocal
obligation:
one could not
exist without
the other.

Clients are the living element that remains in contact, if not with the designer, then at least with the couture house. They are there to remind him that women dress not to cover themselves but to seduce.

It can be said without exaggeration that, for us, our clients are our true collaborators.

A woman's duty towards her couturier is to choose gowns that show her at her best, because those that don't suit her will do a disservice to the name of the house.

Their demands sometimes know no bounds and we would be ruined if we conceded to them all. But I don't want to forget that they have every right, including the right to overstep the mark.

FASHION
ACCORDING TO
DIOR

The spirit of fashion? (It's actually the public who create this spirit.) It is made up of many elements. The first is the zeitgeist, the second is logic, the third is chance, the fourth is the decisions that all the magazines make.

A gown isn't made to be admired on a clothes hanger or on the cover of a magazine, but to be worn with pleasure and ease...

The spirit of novelty is the spirit of fashion.

Fashion is no more frivolous than poetry or song. Centuries pass by and with them, fashion takes on a kind of dignity; it becomes a witness to its time.

Fashion cannot exist
without attention, enthusiasm
and passion.

PASSION

for design…

PASSION

for making… and

PASSION

to keep fashion alive!

It's only through technique that fashion can be profoundly changed.

★

Even in its most extravagant designs, fashion must make sense.

★

Fashion is always right. It has a profound rightness, and those who create it and those who follow it are often unaware of that.

★

Fashion does not need to be immediately accessible; it only has to be present.

★

Fashion evolves when it is driven by desire and changes when pushed by distaste. Weariness suddenly makes it destroy what it once loved. Because the underlying reason for its existence is the desire to seduce and attract, its allure cannot be born from uniformity, which is the mother of boredom. This is why, while there is not perhaps a logic of fashion, there is instead a sensibility that follows two reflexes: rejection or approval.

Fashion goes its own way, and nothing can stop it.

★

To have your eyes open to fashion is a way of being up to date; it is a way to appear forever young.

★

Fashion reflects the times almost before people are aware of it themselves. The well-dressed and fashionable woman is just expressing what everybody has in mind.

★

Women's interest in fashion springs partly from the need to attract attention, and partly because it is human to want something new.

★

Now that rarity has been replaced by novelty, it's now no longer a matter of having the most opulent appearance but the most up to date. Surrounding itself in secrets, taking on a faster seasonal rhythm, more bewildering than in the past, fashion – mysterious and unexpected – has once again become, thanks to its aura of the unknown, one of the last refuges of the marvellous.

Fashion is
a message
that's in
the air.

The world has changed its rhythm.

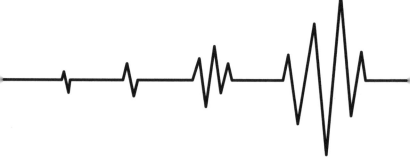

And fashion has changed with it.

The creation of a collection takes two months, therefore fashion must die and die quickly.

★

When fashion propagates and spreads out into the streets, and eventually becomes widespread, it makes itself obsolete.

★

As time passes, things that once were considered ugly are rediscovered with their beauty intact. It is as if fashion gets its posthumous revenge, and even the extravagances of the past will one day regain their charm.

★

It's true that we are viewed as an ephemeral craft. Only the rigour of the construction, the precision of the cut and the quality of the execution separate us from the petticoats.

★

A fashion becomes popular or falls from grace through a complicated series of influences. The most successful fashions go out of style the fastest. This is partly because they are too heavily imitated and therefore grow irrelevant. Only uniforms go out of style slowly.

A change of silhouette, for a couturier, is a delicate affair. He must try to disentangle what people still like from what they no longer like and from what they may like next. New fashion can be found there, at this crossroads on this Carte du Tendre, *and nowhere else.*

★

There's a tendency, you know, to say that I am a revolutionary, but I don't think I am one at all. I take women's fashion back to what it used to be, and I try to show a woman's body to its best advantage, that's all.

★

Fashion is a show of faith. In a century that has attempted to destroy all of its secrets one by one, feeding on false confidences and fabricated revelations, it remains the very embodiment of mystery, and the best proof of its magic is that it has never been so talked about.

Fashion is a means
of expression like any
other, and it's through my
gowns that I have tried,
for my part, to convey
a taste or a feeling.

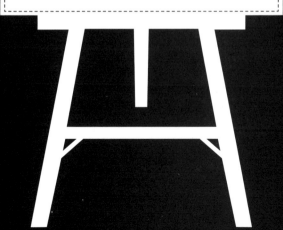

1947

THE NEW LOOK
ACCORDING TO
DIOR

It was the first time that I was working for myself. Absolutely free. And I expressed what I felt deeply.

I must confess that truthfully, of all my collections, it was the inaugural one that required the least effort and caused the least worry. As a matter of fact, I was not running any risk of disappointing the public since they did not know me, had no expectations and made no demands on me.

What was hailed as a new style was only the natural and sincere expression of the fashion I wanted to create.

I RECEIVED A HUGE QUANTITY
OF POST AFTER THE NEW LOOK.
IF SOMEONE'S POPULARITY
CAN BE MEASURED BY
THE WEIGHT OF LETTERS
THEY GET,
I OUGHT TO HAVE
BEEN CONSIDERED
A VERY IMPORTANT PERSON.

**We were
coming out
of a time
of war, of
uniforms,
of soldier-women
built like boxers.**

*I drew
flower-women
with soft shoulders,
generous busts,
waists as slim
as vines and
skirts as wide
as petals.*

The New Look was only a success because it moved in the same direction as the times: an era that was trying to get away from the mechanical and the inhuman, to rediscover tradition and its constants.

As with all eras, our own is seeking a face. The mirror that reveals it cannot be anything other than the mirror of truth. By being natural and sincere, you can start revolutions without even trying.

I am looking at the press release that I wrote back then. It was on a simple typed and photocopied sheet of paper. I described two principal silhouettes: the Corolle and the 8. Elongated skirts, with very defined waists, these deliberately feminine lines were almost immediately christened the New Look.

When the New Look began, it was predicted that, like all cycles in fashion, it would last around seven or eight years. I said it at the time: a fashion generally lasts for seven years.

★

My intention was not to revolutionize fashion, but just to create what I wanted to create. My ideal was to be called a 'good craftsman': a rather understated expression that I like, since it combines honesty and quality.

★

The New Look did not last, because like all revolutions and radical changes, the pendulum had swung too far.

Being responsible for
a new movement,
when I tried to analyse it,
I realized that it was
primarily a revival
of the

ART
OF
PLEASING.

PERFUME ACCORDING TO DIOR

*Of the women of my childhood, I particularly
remember their perfumes, long-lasting perfumes –
much more than those of today – that lingered in
the elevator, well after they had gone.*

*How did I become a perfumer? By chance,
because you know how chance comes to the aid
of people who really want something. Chance was
the meeting of someone with plenty of ideas with
favourable circumstances.*

*For a perfume to catch on, it must first have spent
a long time in the hearts of those who created it.*

*This is why
I became a perfumer
too: so that all I have
to do is remove the
stopper from a
bottle to see all my
dresses wafting out
and so that every
woman I dress
can leave a*

TRAIL OF DESIRE

flowing behind her.

Perfume
is a
vital
asset of
femininity.

Perfume is the indispensable accessory to a woman's personality, it's the finishing touch to a gown, it's the rose that Lancret used to sign his canvases.

It's as important for a woman to have a subtle scent as it is to have elegant outfits.

Just like your clothes, your perfume should express your personality.

It is hard to imagine the care and attention that go into developing a new perfume, designing a bottle, or even some simple packaging. These tasks are so consuming that I consider myself today to be a perfumer as much as a couturier.

We worked and researched, like alchemists seeking the Philosopher's Stone. And then Miss Dior was born. It was born from evenings in Provence, buzzing with fireflies, where the green jasmine sings in harmony with the tune of the night and the earth.

Make me a perfume that smells like love!
[To Paul Vacher, creator of Miss Dior]

SPRAY MORE PERFUME!

[Before his first fashion show,
in the salons of 30 avenue Montaigne, Paris]

DRESSING ACCORDING TO DIOR

It's a sophistication of mind that allows you to dress well, not money.

★

Every ten years a woman should take a clear look at herself.

★

What you need to discover is yourself; find out what suits you, and in which style of clothes you feel happy and comfortable.

★

You cannot use fashion until you know yourself. Good taste is to resemble oneself.

★

Above all, good taste in clothes is to appear natural.

First of all,
look at yourself
in the mirror,
and decide what
age you are. What
age you want to look.
And what age
you truly believe
you *can* look.

It's not the

quantity

but the

quality

and care of your
clothes that will
create an effect.

I am sure that it is far easier for a woman to keep herself elegant if she doesn't try to have too many clothes. It is much better to have a minimal but complete wardrobe of the best quality that you can possibly buy. That is to say, having a suitable outfit for each of life's occasions.

One of the greatest advantages of a restricted wardrobe is that you avoid the serious risk of overdoing it. The worst way to spend your money is to buy lots of cheap clothes. The fleeting pleasure of wearing something just because it's new will soon fade, and you'll find yourself with a dress or a suit that quickly loses its shape and its charm.

Although she may not have everything she wants, a woman who really knows how to dress can put together a perfect wardrobe even without a huge number of dresses, because she has a style.

I am constantly asked if I would advise a woman to change her appearance from time to time. My answer is an apparent contradiction: I would say to her: 'Always be yourself, but change the way you look.'

★

Good taste is nothing more than the ability to select things that suit your personality and are appropriate to your particular way of life. It is to adapt fashionable items to fit your own wardrobe.

★

Never let a woman say that gowns by X or Y aren't made for her and don't suit her, because there are enough gowns in any collection for all varieties of female beauty. All you need is to know how to choose them, to know yourself, to know how to look in a mirror and seek out the image not of the woman you'd like to be, but the woman that you are.

The essence of being well-dressed? To dress simply. To make the best of one's good points and to

camouflage the bad ones.

Avoid
eccentricity,
but be brave
enough to
adopt anything
new that
is obviously
flattering
to you.

*The woman who is at the vanguard of fashion
is only visually expressing what everybody else
has in mind. She looks the way other women would
like to look – if only they knew it.*

★

*I do not advise women to stick too closely to
'classic styles'. To be eternally classic is to be
dreadfully dull.*

★

*Being chic doesn't necessarily mean wearing
a different outfit every day.*

★

*I hate more than anything to see a woman who
looks overdressed.*

DIOR
ACCORDING TO
CHRISTIAN

That obscure word

'business'

with all the
formidable
vagueness
that it suggests,
has always
terrified me.

I am not the fashion dictator that so many people describe. I cannot decree what women ought to wear, no more so than anyone else. All that we can do is make suggestions.

The dreaded professional gaze… It seems I must possess this gaze. I have to confess that I can never switch it off. I am told that women feel undressed when confronted by it. They are wrong: I am simply trying to imagine them dressed differently.

It's this dreaded professional gaze that prevents me from complimenting a pretty woman that I have dressed: it would sound like I was partly congratulating myself for her success.

The one thing that I think is vital, even in the greatest luxury: simplicity.

The crazy pin-up, publicity-hungry starlet style is over now. We need to find something else. Mistakes always get a reaction.

It has been my lot to provoke a lot of comments through no intention of my own. I'm not trying to innovate, I'm just doing what I feel. But perhaps sincerity is the rarest and most revolutionary thing there is.

Personally, I don't like too much sophistication, I prefer a more natural look.

★

Fantasy for the sake of fantasy, excess for the sake of excess: those things smack of costume, not couture.

$$\left(\begin{array}{c} \text{Don't expect too much} \\ \text{from me. I'm against} \\ \text{exaggeration in any form.} \end{array} \right)$$

For me,

EVERYTHING

changes
and

NOTHING

has
changed.

I have a reactionary temperament, a term that's too often confused with 'regressive'.

We never look back and our job is to create pleasure by moving forwards.

A design must both perpetuate and surprise.
As a piece of clothing, it should respect custom;
as an outfit, it should dare to be bold. It combines
audacity with tradition.

I wanted to prove wrong that oft-heard, worrying phrase: 'You can't do that any more.' I refused to accept that the battle was already lost and I believe that in any era, if someone wanted to create something worthwhile, they would have done the same. Rare are the moments in history where people have been carried along by the current of the century and have never had a reason to speak out against it.

I am wary of anything that is easy. The ideal rules that constrain the poet and the practical necessities that restrict the architect have never stopped him from being inspired. On the contrary, they focus him and prevent him from distraction.

Our watchword is maintenance:
maintaining

TRADITIONS

of quality, traditions which,
admittedly, do not always complement
the current state of the world and the
means available to everyone, but
maintaining them nonetheless,
in spite of everything, trying to find
a place for them and integrating
them into the network of modern
techniques. Why are we doing this?
To pass on these traditions to the
generations that will follow.

*A nice, peaceful,
country life…
that's the life I love.*

*An extraordinary feeling grips me every time
I return home. Nothing beats coming back to one's
own land, and I pity those who don't have enough
ties to a community to feel it.*

★

*When only a few steps away from my vines and
my jasmines, close to the soil, I always feel more
at ease.*

★

I wanted to make this house [the Château de la
Colle Noire] *into my real home. A place where
I could close the loop of my existence and
rediscover, in another setting, the protected garden
of my childhood. A place where I can finally live in
peace, forgetting Christian Dior and becoming just
Christian again.*

Decoration and architecture are my first vocations.

★

I retain the warmest and most wonderful memories of the house I grew up in. What can I say? My life and my style owe almost everything to its location and its architecture.

★

Living in a house that isn't anything like you is a little like wearing someone else's clothes.

★

At the risk of sounding like a monster, I must admit that if I didn't like houses so much then dresses would be my entire existence.

By describing its shell you define a snail.

We only express a thing

well

when we understand it

well.

Being hard on oneself can be as dangerous as excessive indulgence.

We all have a weakness. It's our strength. It sustains us through the tedium of the daily grind and gives us a good excuse for our material success, which is that it has earned us the means to satisfy it.

Like the goddess of Fortune, the goddess of Publicity smiles on those who court her the least.

You have every right to make mistakes, as long as you are doing something you love; on the other hand, doing something you don't enjoy is unforgivable, especially if it brings success.

My favourite motto of all: I shall endure.

★

Are we optimists? Dreamers? Utopians? Perhaps. And we are glad to be so.

★

I am demanding. One should always be if you are in the business of turning dreams into a reality.

★

My dream is to dress the Christian Dior woman from head to toe.

I am a
mild man,
but I have
violent
TASTES.

SOURCES

BOOKS

Christian Dior, *Christian Dior et moi*
(Paris: Vuibert, 2011)

Christian Dior, *Je suis couturier* (Paris: Éditions du
Conquistador, 1951)

Christian Dior, 'Petit dictionnaire de la mode', in *Dior – 60
années hautes en couleur* (Paris: ArtLys, 2007)

Christian Dior, 'Conversation with Alice Perkins and Lucie
Noël, 10 January 1955', Paris, in *Les Années 50, la mode en
France 1947–1957* (Paris: Paris-Musées, 2014)

*Conférences écrites par Christian Dior pour la Sorbonne
1955–1957* (Paris: Institut Français de la Mode – Éditions
du Regard, 2003)

Cecil Beaton, *Cinquante ans d'élégance et d'art de vivre*
(Paris: Séguier, 2017)

Célia Bertin, *Haute Couture, terre inconnue*
(Paris: Hachette, 1956)

Chapeaux Dior! De Christian Dior à Stephen Jones (Paris,
Rizzoli Flammarion, 2020)

Marcel Jullian, *Délit de vagabondage* (Paris: Grasset, 1978)

Les parfums Christian Dior (Musée de Granville, 1987)

MAGAZINES AND NEWSPAPERS

Aurore
Elle
Hull Daily Mail
Jardin des Modes
Life
Modern Woman
New York Herald Tribune
Woman's Home Companion
Woman's Illustrated

INTERVIEWS

Institut national de l'audiovisuel (INA)
Person to Person, CBS
Radio Genève
Radio Télévision Française (RTF)

ABOUT THE AUTHORS

A writer, editor and journalist, Patrick Mauriès has published numerous books and essays on art, literature, fashion and the decorative arts. He has written books on a range of figures including Jean-Paul Goude, Christian Lacroix and Karl Lagerfeld.

Jean-Christophe Napias is an author, publisher and editor. He has written several books on Paris (including *Quiet Corners of Paris*) and has edited works on French literature.

Patrick Mauriès and Jean-Christophe Napias have previously co-authored titles including *Choupette: The Private Life of a High Flying Fashion Cat*, *Fashion Quotes* and *The World According to Karl* and *The World According to Coco* in this series.